Seasons in Mind: Celebrating the Solstices

Jim Donovan

Pine Meadow Partners, LLC

P.O. Box 243

Keyport, NJ 07735

Cover Art by Harriman Donovan

Print ISBN 978-0-57841-749-3

eBook ISBN 978-1-54397-019-7

Dedicated to
Emilia and Harry

Contents

Introduction

Consider the fact that one day you came to "be." In a relative flash on the scale of all human history, first you were non-existent, then sperm met egg, and you developed and then were born, like the rest of us, on our Earth. Being born from the elements of our Earth, and all life on Earth emanating from the energy of light and warmth of the Sun through photosynthesis, brings us to the importance of the Solstices.

The whole idea of Solstice is to be cognizant of a moment: the now. The moment of Solstice represents a starting point, from which many paths radiate. Celebrating Solstice is the culmination of our beliefs because it is the celebration of the moment: the moment each of us "became," the moment we each started on the journey of our own arc, and is a celebration of our relationship to the Sun. In the mechanism of the elliptical dance of the Earth with the Sun, there is the apogee and the perigee, like the high points of swinging on a swingset. Could we let that moment just pass and exist unaware?—sure, but if it's representative of something deeper or more complex, then why not use it as a focal point to celebrate the truth of our existence?

Acknowledging the moments of the Solstices, those extremes in the elliptical orbit of our Earth around the Sun, offers us yet another opportunity to express gratitude for those people and things that allow stability for our individual well-being. It also lends us "pause" to consider our reliance on others and the wonders of our oneness.

Though our celebrations of the Solstices herald from the age of early modern humans, of the so-called "pagans," our perspective is formed by the accumulated knowledge and discoveries of every age that finds us now in the 21st century. Obviously, we know much more than the generations of the past generally could have known or been aware of. However, this is not to say that they, in many ways, did not know more or were less aware than we about many, many things. It was a sense of wonder and the instinct of many individuals of the past which enabled us to have such a presently relatively enlightened perspective.

While we as a species have made so many marvelous discoveries and have made so much technological and scientific progress over the last few hundred years, there are still many mysteries to wonder about. Even the most highly educated geniuses still do not know yet the true nature of the universe, or multi-universes, or multi-dimensions of space and time—they are still philosophizing and exist in a state of wonder. Therefore, this ability to wonder is the human quality or condition that is the greatest equalizer of all of humanity.

Our traditions and celebrations described in this book offer an opportunity to pause and reflect on all that we now know and all that we still do not know about our universe. We contemplate our heliosphere and our natural world's dependence upon the cycles of the Earth and Sun. The readings and activities described provide a framework for celebrating what we know about these cycles and for sharing with others our curiosity about what we still have yet to learn, in so doing inspiring a sense of wonder about our universe and our place within it.

Our acknowledgement and celebrations of the Solstices have been, and continue to be, evolving—just as it will be so for you. Our group has expanded through the years, starting as a small gathering of very close friends seeking ways to bring the quality of daily awareness and meaning into their lives. The expansion is a result of our children inviting interested friends, as well as close friends inviting their interested friends or family. For many the experience of celebrating the Solstices, and of becoming more aware of the equinoxes and the daily change through the course of each year, has lent a fresher perspective on their inherited religions, with their various demands, requirements, obligations, and "observances."

We hope to offer here a framework of activities, and we hope that you will personalize and enhance this structure so that the Solstices bring meaning and a clearer perspective into your lives and the lives of your friends and loved ones. And remember, we here at the Donovan household, wherever we are, will be acknowledging those moments of the Solstices at the precise time that you are celebrating these moments. We raise our hearts and minds together.

The Wreath

A focal point of our celebrations and rituals is the wreath

Our Wreath at Summer Solstice

On a cold Saturday morning in late February or early March, with smoke rising from the workshop woodstove white against the dark grey sky, I go out to the grape arbor. All its leaves have been shed, and a thick criss-crossing of vines and canes and tendrils clings overhead. I first built the arbor in 1994 with sought-after locust trees that I found and downed in the nearby woods; locust wood holds up well in the ground and against the natural elements. The arbor is covered with the vines of several grape plants we have acquired over the years, mostly a wild concord variety. In summer, we enjoy the shade of the large grape leaves, sitting under the arbor built to enable passage of a car, even an SUV. Now, my goal is to begin the process of creating our Solstice Wreath, later to be decorated with wild flowers as part of our Summer Solstice celebration, and then ultimately to be burned in a campfire as part of our Winter Solstice celebration. The wreath forms the centerpiece, both literally and symbolically, of our yearly traditions.

Why the Wreath?

The wreath is a symbol of the connectivity of all things and a symbol of each of our continuing reliance on the whole. It is the cynosure of our celebrations throughout the year, valued by all of us for its embodiment of the melding of artistic craftsmanship and the beauty of Nature. Its circular structure represents the enduring Sun and the cycle of its planets, as well as the unity of all things in the universe.

So, if you want to create your own wreath out of grapevine, you'll need a source. If you are fortunate enough to live near wooded areas where concord grapes grow wild, you may have an abundant source there. However, oftentimes, the vines are so old that the reachable vines are very thick, and the ones you need may be thriving a ways up in the canopy. And so, you may be fortunate to have enough open outdoor space available to you to grown your own. In this way it can be assured that the vines are just thick and supple enough to use after a season's growth.

The resistance of the Locust tree to decay is due to chemicals that it produces that are toxic to some forms of life, particularly insects and fungi. Native Americans used the pods as a purgative. There has been research done to try and isolate the tree's toxic chemicals, for potential use as natural wood preservatives. High concentrations of a flavenoid called robinetin and a fungal growth inhibitor called taxifolin are thought to play a role. Interestingly, parts of the locust tree are consumed as food by both humans and animals.

E.D.

We have a very simple arrangement: I built an arbor out of the locust trees I harvested from the wooded lot behind our house; my neighbor, the owner of the lot, was happy to allow me to cut down some healthy representatives of this invasive species of tree. Fact is, however, black locust has been used for fence posts for centuries due to their resilience in the soil; they just don't seem to want to decompose! There is an oil in the wood that helps it to resist weathering. This makes for great firewood and fire-starting "fat wood," as it splits very easily and burns very hot. Unfortunately, it's not a fragrant fire the way oak, cherry, or apple wood smells so beautiful on the winter air. Both black locust (Robinia pseudoacacia) and honey locust (Gleditsia triacanthos) seem to offer the same advantages when used for structural posts, but the black locust is most prevalent in the North-East, and it is easily distinguished from the honey locust by its deeply furrowed grayish bark and the lack of very long and sharp thorns in the trunk. The black locust also produces much smaller seed pods than the honey locust. I look for trees that have a good Y shape above a fairly straight section below that is approximately 11.5 to 12 feet/4 meters long , and approximately 6-7 inches/15-17 cm in diameter. The posts will be set 2 to 2.5 feet/.75 meters in the ground. I used six such posts, setting the Y approximately 9 feet/3 meters high, 7 feet/2 meters apart. I then located two 15 foot/4.5-meter-long sections into the top Y's, and then collected 12 young trees, approximately 3-3.5 in/8 cm diameter, and set them perpendicularly across the two long sections top sections. You can imagine why, until the arbor is covered with vines, my neighbor described it as looking like a Native American (or Viking) funeral pyre.

Original Arbor built in 1994

New Arbor built in 2016
using pressure-treated lumber

Once built, it was time to grow grapes. I transplanted four plants from the nearby woods one day in early spring while the vines were still dormant. These four were all concord, but it turns out that one of those plants has produced grapes one inch/2.25 cm in diameter! Very large! We also purchased two grape plants: one seedless red and one seedless white. The thing to remember about grape vines, however, is that they need light. This is why wine-making grape growers only allow root stock to grow upward about four feet, with two arms on each side growing out to about six feet. Constriction leads to fruition. In our case, with six plants growing upwards undeterred, it's lucky if we can keep the grass alive under all of the shade, never mind produce any grapes. But, we grow it for the vines, and we're never disappointed. Every year we have enough vines to make at least three wreaths—very large, thick, heavy wreaths. And so, besides the Solstice wreath, which will meet its fiery and solemn end, we have other wreaths to share or decorate for other more traditional holidays and theme wreaths, like wine cork decorated wreaths, seed package decorated wreaths, or cigar label wreaths—anything you can think of, really.

By late February/early March, the plants have been absent of leaves for the past few months. We could have decided to cut the grape vines and make the wreath on the Spring Equinox of March 21st; however, the vines must be cut while the plants are still in the dormant state, and oftentimes, by March 21st, the grapevines are already budding out. So, we end up cutting the vines somewhere during mid-to-late February or the first week of March and making the wreath then, but then acknowledging the Spring Equinox by placing the wreath in a prominent place in our sun porch, whereupon it will dry out to a great extent by the time Summer Solstice comes around on June 21st, when it will be festooned with the local flora.

Newly made wreaths

Certainly, you can make a wreath out of other plant materials. However, there is something celebratory, maybe Bacchanalian, about the grape vines, the way they produce those spiraling whips, the tendrils which seem to represent the very essence of struggling to survive, of holding on, reaching, climbing. To observe the progress of grape vine tendrils, the plant almost seems sentient, the way it reaches straight out until it touches something and then, serpent-like, coils around it to support the weight of the growing plant.

Grapevines in Summer

But, again, you could use other plants. Wisteria, honeysuckle, and bittersweet vines are commonly used to make wreaths as well. You could use some supple twig-thick branches from many kinds of plants, but you will probably have to weave with much shorter lengths, as only a vine will have long and almost uniform widths.

Symbolism of Vines

Grapes: This vine is associated with the Greek god Dionysus (Roman god Bacchus), the god of wine. He is also the god of festivity and merry-making and was considered the patron god of the arts.

Honeysuckle: The vine's sweet flowers are associated with love. During the Victorian era, suitors gave honeysuckle flowers as a promise of true love. It is referenced throughout literature as symbol of romantic love and physical attraction.

Willow: The branch of this tree has significance in many cultures (Jewish, Chinese, Japanese, English). The tree is used to produce salicylic acid, an ingredient in aspirin. It is associated with healing and peaceful rest.

Wisteria: This incredibly strong vine is associated with endurance and boundless creative energy, but energy that must be kept in check. It produces beautiful, highly fragrant flowers.

All of these plants produce vines and branches that are sturdy and durable, making them perfect for wreaths. The plants themselves are hearty and grow with vigor, and so, when tamed so as to form the wreath's unbroken circle, they represent Nature's own endurance throughout the cycle of the year.

Making the wreath is an arduous process. I will position a ladder beside the arbor and try to locate vines that are growing near the top, cut them each one at a time and place them in sections on the lawn according to thickness and length. If I notice any lengths that have particularly attractive/artistic looking hardy tendrils, those curly, spirally whip-like structures which enable the vine to cling and climb, I will set a stash of them aside so as not to damage the tendrils; short sections with the tendrils can be weaved-in later in the process, and it's very unlikely that the best tendrils will be exposed and artistic-looking after the wrestling match of making the wreath. To collect the best and most visually appealing tendrils, I cut the vines leaving approximately four inches (10 cm) on <u>each</u> side of each tendril. I make an oblique or pointed cut in doing so; this enables me to weave the tendril into the finished wreath, and it will appear to be a fortuitously seamless placement, aesthetically pleasing to the eye.

So, I continue that process of cutting the long vines one at a time, from top to bottom, pulling it out of the great tangle, assessing, and then setting aside, in groups by length, thickness or tendril potential. I will try to leave one or two relatively long vines on the end of each of the six plants as grapes will only grow from the year-old vines. So, even if it's unlikely that we will get to enjoy much of fruit, I give it a try even so.

*According to Washington State University Extension: "Grapes bear fruit on the green shoots that arise from **one-year-old canes**"*

Now comes the fun part. There are several methods one can use to create a wreath of grape vines. You could choose to begin by using some sort of circular armature. However, once the time comes to burn the wreath, the appearance of this armature, whether made of thick wire or bended metal tubing, detracts from the visual experience of the burning process. So, too, one could simply coil the vine like any rope or electrical cord and then wrap it with wires or twine, but here again, the effect is diminished when either the wreath begins to unwind (over time or as a result of the fire when your hemp twine burns through) or hot, glowing wires appear when the wreath is burned. The process I have adopted to create the wreath has been described as a "wrestling match," and, I have to say, it is a bit of work. However, the end product, so tightly wound, so spiral, thick and substantive, lends itself to an experience similar to the burning of the Yule log. For, if the wreath is merely coiled, the space between the vines is allowed so much oxygen that the structure, having been drying since February, and the decorative wildflowers drying since Summer Solstice, will burn almost explosively and rapidly and hot. This detracts from the burning experience as it creates concern, and likely fear, as the wreath catches fire, quickly and violently burning out in a few minutes, if not seconds, and allowing little time to toss in the "burden" (see chapter on "The Winter Solstice").

For a video of this wreath-making process or for how you can buy one of our wreaths, see our website seasonsinmind.com

I start by taking one of the longest lengths of vine and, starting from the thick-wood end, creating one circle, imagining the diameter of this circle to be the inner-most heart of the eventual ring. Now, it's a matter of reaching into the ring and pulling the rest of the vine through, wrapping that section at a particular angle, not too acute and not too obtuse, around the outside of the ring and pulling through again. So, it is essentially a continual spiral, and I try to pull it tight as I can at every step, thus assuring the making of a very dense and very heavy wreath. Once the moisture in the vines evaporates over ten months' time (from now, through the Summer Solstice when it will be decorated with wildflowers, to the Winter Solstice), the wreath will have lost most of this water weight. But, the tight construction will make for a slow and lasting burn which will lend itself to the lengthening of a very somber and solemn experience at the Winter Solstice fire.

You may wonder: should the wreath be wrapped right to left or left to right? Well, in space there is no North or South; looking at Earth from the north pole, it spins counter-clockwise, from the south, clock-wise. Also, my guide would be, whether you are left-handed or right-handed, go with what feels natural to you. It won't be easy either way, so try to enjoy the process. This is part of the motivation for creating the wreath in late February: it's still chilly outside! But, engaging in this process will get you to break a sweat. As you come to the end of a particular length of vine, you will use the last foot and a half (45 cm) to weave-in the next length, thus weaving each end into the beginning of the next length. Most imperfect weavings will be forgiven as you continue to overlap with the other lengths.

Making the Wreath

When you are satisfied with the size and girth of your wreath, it's time to weave the end of the final length onto the ring. There might be two to four ends to tie into the wreath. I take hand clippers and make an oblique or pointed cut at the end. Then, push about three inches (7.5 cm), or as much as can be forced, back into the dense weave. I do this with each end until all of the vines are inextricably intertwined. Now, I go back to the stash of tendrils: the curly whip-like structures that enable the grape vines to climb. I decide where I'd like to place the curly-q and force the two pointed ends of that vine into the wreath as though it is aligned and a contiguous part of the spiral pattern of the wreath. Finally, I take hand clippers and snip off any extruding ends or segments of the outer vine bark that may have come free during the twisting weave process.

Final steps

The last step is to find a dry, hopefully interior location for the beautiful creation. Looking to the future, one can imagine how difficult it will be, how downcast and crest-fallen we will be, to touch a lighted match to this much-earned artistic creation. One can think of it as a personal sacrifice, an act of service, respect, and wonder toward the truly awesome and profound nature and workings of our life-sustaining solar system, and toward the humanly unfathomable vastness of the Universe. One can meditate on the symbol of the unbroken circle, the tangible expression of the cycles which occur all around us: in our bodies, in our relationships, in our societies, and in our entire lives. And for now, the wreath will serve as a reminder of the days to come and of the wondrous truths that frame our lives. Remember, after all, the ephemeral nature of every flower, indeed of every life.

Once completed, on March 21st the wreath is ceremoniously hung in our sun porch or hung on a sheltered wall on the outside of the workshop. It's as if the newly warm days and the still-cold nights make the wreath more hardy. It sits, almost majestically, as if awaiting the longest day of Summer. It's beautiful on its own, but come Summer Solstice, it will be transformed. The vines must age and mellow, cure, if you will, as they come to accept the unnatural twists and turns into which they have been forced. The heavy moisture slowly evaporates, the internal tension seems to cease: acceptance in having been shaped and tamed.

Undecorated Wreath before the final trimming

Wreath Decorated after Summer Solstice

The Summer Solstice

Celebrating the Longest Day

When we celebrate the Summer Solstice, we are getting together to celebrate the longest day and take advantage of the long hours of sunlight.

Our Summer Solstice Celebration Includes:

- Waking to watch the sunrise
- Sharing a breakfast
- Gathering wildflowers
- Decorating the Solstice Wreath
- Activities/afternoon walk
- Summer Solstice dinner
- Writing of our wishes and the Summer Solstice fire

The word "solstice" literally means "the Sun stands still." Have you noticed how, year after year, from the first blooms of spring to the beginning of summer, the Sun seems to be moving toward the North (higher overhead, rising more toward the Northeast, setting more Northwest) a bit more every day? Then it seems to stop heading North, just as summer begins. During another portion of the year, as the children begin a new school year in September, the Sun seems to be moving South (rising more and more toward the Southeast and setting more Southwest) but then stops heading South. The days become either longer or shorter as the Sun is either higher or lower in the sky at noon. The more north, the Sun's higher in the sky, and the longer the day; the more south, the Sun low in the Southern sky, the shorter the day. Just notice how long your shadow is on a sunny day at noon in winter, whereas in summer at noon, you hardly have a shadow at all! This is because the Earth is tilting in relation to the Sun at an angle of 23.5 degrees. ("this angle is known as the *obliquity of the ecliptic* and is the cause of the seasons on Earth" *National Audubon Society Field Guide to the Night Sky*). The Earth retains this angle because it acts as a giant gyroscope, the Northern Hemisphere sometimes tilting *toward* the Sun (in summer) and sometimes tilting *away* from the Sun (in winter). The more direct the Sun's rays on the Earth, the hotter that area, whether land or sea. This is why, during the Summer, the Sun is almost perfectly directly overhead to the extent that a flagpole would have very little shadow. Whereas in Winter, for the Northern Hemisphere, the Sun traverses our Southern skies, from south-east to south-west, thus creating *long* shadows at noon.

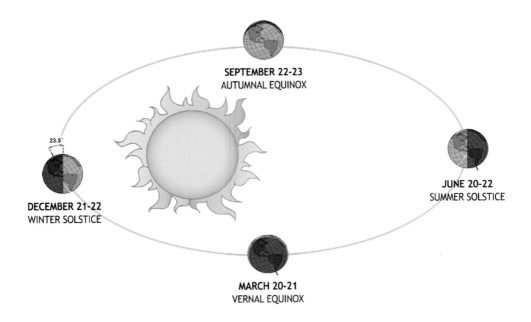

Illustration by Harriman Donovan

Earth's Orbit around the Sun
Painting by Jim T. Donovan

Summer Solstice (for the Northern Hemisphere) occurs on or about June 21st when the Sun reaches a latitude of approximately 23.5 degrees, in the so-called "Tropic of Cancer." This is its most northerly position from our perspective. In the Northern Hemisphere, the Summer Solstice is the longest day. The day and precise moment, down to the minute, of Summer Solstice could very easily come and go without being acknowledged, more so than for the Winter Solstice because for the winter, you're dying for the days to get longer. During winter, many can't wait for the warmer days to arrive. Summer Solstice, on the other hand, is seen by most as merely "the first day of summer," and some may willfully overlook the fact that, although the summer is just beginning, the days are already getting shorter, albeit slowly, incrementally. So, although we first began celebrating Winter Solstice, we also wanted to acknowledge Summer Solstice and its place in the cycle. When we get to June 21st, there is almost a feeling of irony because, from here on, the days are getting shorter.

Daisy declares in *The Great Gatsby*: "In two weeks, it will be the longest day of the year. . . . Do you always look for the longest day of the year and then miss it? I always watch for the longest day in the year and then miss it"

Counter-intuitively, in the Northern Hemisphere, the Earth in its elliptical orbit around the Sun is actually at its <u>farthest point</u> (aphelion) <u>away from the Sun</u> at the *Summer* Solstice! One would think that if the Earth is at its *farthest* position from the Sun, the Earth would be cooler. But, because of Earth's tilt, the Northern Hemisphere, facing toward the Sun, experiences summer, and the beginning of the hottest days. Although the Sun is at its most northerly point as we see it, directly overhead on approx. June 21st, the Northern Hemisphere does not completely warm until the oceans and land have had time to warm. This is why the Northern Hemisphere experiences its greatest heat in July and August, through jet-streaming wind patterns and warming oceans, just as January and February tend to be colder than December 21st, the *Winter* Solstice, as it takes time for the land masses and oceans to cool.

The Moment of Solstice:

Whether we are gathering on the actual Solstice or on a day near the Solstice, we always try to be cognizant of the moment in the transition in the cycle. Depending upon when it occurs in our celebration, we might have a moment of silence through the transition and then have readings or a song or light a candle. If the moment of Summer Solstice occurs during the actual day of our celebration, we will try to organize our day around being together at the fire at the moment of Solstice or being engaged in one of the important steps in the celebration at that moment. We always know when the actual moment of Solstice is, and, it's perfect if we can be together at that moment. But, people have busy lives, occupations, etc., so sometimes we cannot be together. Therefore, we make sure we always acknowledge the moment of transition somehow.

Remember when you were a kid and coming inside as late as 9 or 9:30 pm in summertime and how good that felt? With modern obligations and concerns, the rigid, unchanging nature of our work and daily schedules does not conform to the variations of the rhythmical ebb and flow of daylight and darkness over the course of a year.

Dates and Times of the Solstices 2019-2029

Eastern Standard Time--Daylight Saving Time conversion is <u>not</u> included

Solstice	2019 Jun 21 Fri	10:54
Solstice	2019 Dec 21 Sat	23:19
Solstice	2020 June 20 Sat	16:43
Solstice	2020 Dec 21 Mon	5: 02
Solstice	2021 Jun 20 Sun	22:32
Solstice	2021 Dec 21 Tues	10:59
Solstice	2022 Jun 21 Tues	4:14
Solstice	2022 Dec 21 Wed	16:48
Solstice	2023 Jun 21 Wed	9:58
Solstice	2023 Dec 21 Thurs	22:27
Solstice	2024 Jun 20 Thurs	15:51
Solstice	2024 Dec 21 Sat	4:20
Solstice	2025 Jun 20 Fri	21:42
Solstice	2025 Dec 21 Sun	10:03
Solstice	2026 Jun 21 Sun	3:24
Solstice	2026 Dec 21 Mon	15:50
Solstice	2027 Jun 21 Mon	9:11
Solstice	2027 Dec 21 Tues	21:42
Solstice	2028 Jun 20 Tues	15:02
Solstice	2028 Dec 21 Thurs	3:19
Solstice	2029 Jun 20 Wed	20:48
Solstice	2029 Dec 21 Fri	9:14

Solstice Sunrise and Breakfast

We want to acknowledge the Summer Solstice as it represents part of the continuing cycle in Earth's relationship to our life-giving Sun. We thought of ways that it would contrast with our winter-time celebration. Part of our Winter celebration entails our shedding burdens [see Winter Solstice], so for Summer, we focus on our hopes. The Summer Solstice celebration is like a glorified picnic and/or barbecue; it's a lot of people, old friends as well as newcomers, getting together, being outside. Like most parties, a lot of our celebration revolves around an abundance of food and drink. By the time June 21st comes around, there are greens and snap peas and beans galore in the garden. Strawberries are also ready to be picked. Because we are celebrating the longest day, we try to take advantage of the full day, because from here on the days will be getting shorter. Many of the day's activities are active rather than quiet and reflective, in contrast to the Winter Solstice celebration which is simpler, more ascetic and more contemplative.

We start off the day by trying to catch the sunrise—which is difficult because the day is so long, and the Sun rises *so early*! So, it's a matter of setting your alarm and making plans ahead of time to find a place in the East where the Sun will be breaching the most north-eastern horizon at its rising. From this day on, you can mark the Sun rising a little more south of the north-eastern compass point. (There will be a delay of a few days, of course, before this change occurs. Again, the Sun has "stopped" moving North of the East compass point before it starts to move toward East, which it will reach on the sunrise of the Equinox.)

For us, the best view is at the beach on the Jersey Shore. So, essentially, you want to get to the highest point in your area, whether it's a hill, or a mountain, or a high-rise building—or, if you're on an eastern coast, it's the seaside. Bring your sunglasses and be careful not to look directly at the Sun. Weather is always a crap-shoot, but often-times, the minutes before the actual Sun's peaking over the horizon can be very brilliant and spectacular. Keep in mind, however, that as you see the light come over the horizon, what you are actually seeing is an optical illusion caused by light being bent by the Earth's atmosphere and gravity—the lensing effect. This phenomenon holds true as well for sunset. The colors in the sky at sunrise and sunset these days are profoundly affected by particles in the air, but the resulting colors can be astounding.

Summer Solstice at the beach

The saying "red sky at night, sailors delight; red sky at morning, sailors give warning" often holds true. So, if you're lucky enough to have a spectacular sunrise, you might be experiencing some rain later on. If it turns out that the weather is poor (or end-of-school-year events preclude having a day-long celebration), you can find another day close to Summer Solstice. If you want to celebrate it, in addition to just being conscious of it, then you can be conscious of it on the actual day and even the moment and celebrate it on a day that is approximal. It's much easier to watch the sunrises during the equinoxes because the Sun rises at a much more reasonable time—say 6:45 am—whereas for the Summer Solstice sunrise is usually approximately 5:25 am!

Depending upon where you are for the sunrise, afterward, you can go someplace that's open early for breakfast or enjoy the morning at the beach or a park, perhaps bringing a picnic breakfast. At breakfast, we share a reading.

Excerpt from George Meredith's poem "The Longest Day:"

'Tis the longest, the longest of all the glad year,
The longest in life and the fairest in hue,
When day and night, in bridal light,
Mingle their beings beneath the sweet blue,
And bless the balmy air!

Upward to this starry height
The culminating seasons rolled;
On one slope the green with spring delight,
The other with harvest gold,
And treasures of Autumn untold:
And on this highest throne of the   midsummer now
The waning but deathless day doth dream,
With a rapturous grace, as tho' from the face
Of the unveiled infinity, lo, a far beam
Had fall'n on her dim-flushed brow!
. . .
Ye summer souls, raise up one voice!
A charm is afloat all over the land;
The ripe year doth fall to the Spirit of all,
Who blesses it with outstretched hand;
Ye summer souls, rejoice!

Other possible poems to use:

"The Longest Day" by William Wordsworth

"The Summer Sun Shone Round Me" by Robert Louis Stevenson

"Summer in the South" by Paul Laurence Dunbar

"The Summer Day" by Mary Oliver

Gathering Wildflowers and Decorating the Wreath

After breakfast, it's time to focus on decorating the wreath, our most important Summer Solstice tradition. The symbol of the wreath, the unbroken circle, symbolizes the year. So, while we create the wreath itself in February or March, we acknowledged the Summer Solstice by decorating the wreath with wildflowers in bloom on June 21st. Early on, we decide when and where we will go to gather wildflowers to use to decorate the wreath. We try to schedule it so that as many people can join in the search for and collection of flowers. Most times after breakfast, we take a little road trip to a predetermined promising location for finding the greatest variety of wildflowers and tall grasses. The point is the gathering of friends and family who are available to come together to acknowledge the approaching celestial event, to be out in Nature in a place where views are expansive and where there is no cement or blacktop around, only fields, trees and an occasional barn or some such.

We are fortunate to live within a short distance of several farms open to the public and parks with large open fields where we can go. Of course, for those who live in more urban settings, keep in mind that some of the most beautiful "wildflowers" are technically weeds, and one might be amazed at the variety of colors, shapes, and sizes you can find growing in local parks and undeveloped lots and even in cracks in the sidewalk, from chicory to bayflower to queen anne's lace, black-eyed suzies, daisies, coreopsis, some clover, some sunflowers. Also, you can pick some tall grass seed heads of rye or some of the milkweed flower heads or some of the unripe blackberry or raspberry buds which are very bright purply-red or maroon. We are looking for a variation of color, shapes, and an aesthetically pleasing combination of wild plants. Though there are seldom enough flower clippers to go around for each of us, casual groups naturally form as friends get to catch up or others create new acquaintances. Some have to carry a bag or basket, but this is never a burden. We clip as much of the greenery from the flowers as possible, as most leaves will not dry in an aesthetically pleasing way. Whereas the flowers often retain much of their original colors, the leaves sadly wilt, brown up and tend to crumble. Usually, after getting the flowers, we converge at home to decorate the wreath. The actual decorating of the wreath is much like creating a flower *arrangement* and in our case is a group creation, so it is not one singular aesthetic creation. We generally determine together what the top of the wreath will be and flare the flowers outward from there.

Decorating the Wreath

Finished Wreath

Now that it's decorated, you'll want to hang it in a place that's sufficiently dry, in an indoor place that is still and where you can all enjoy it. We usually keep it where everyone can see it on that Summer Solstice day, but then put it in our sunporch to stay out to dry until Winter Solstice.

Activities

After finishing the wreath, we engage in some activities. These can include making flower headdresses or friendship bracelets. These things can be made from long wide iris leaves, long braided flower stems, colored threads or bendable wire with cloth flowers.

We have also made sun dials with the children. To make these, I will locate a tree limb, usually of maple or birch, that is approximately 4 inches/10 cm in diameter, and which will be as circular as possible when cross-cut. I will use a handsaw to cut the branch to a length of about two to two-and-a half feet. Then I use a miter saw to cut discs of 3/8"/2.5 cm thickness. Then, for each disc, I'll use a drill to create a pilot hole approximately ½" from the edge. Into this hole I'll set a "finishing nail" of approximately 1 ½" to 1 ¾" length. Using a compass, we set the disc down on a level surface in a sunny location and have the nail be standing directly southward. As we reach the top of each hour, we trace a line in the shadow of the nail. At the end of the day, you have a working sundial!

These activities have been appropriate for every age group, from pre-kindergarten to grandparents. In addition, if the group is a little older, we will share our time together on an afternoon hike or will go someplace for a swim.

See seaonsinmind.com for more activities

Sun dials

Summer Solstice Dinner

After a swim or a hike, we stop on the way home to pick up soft-shell crab, having ordered it ahead of time. The symbolism of the crab derives from the fact that, in the Summer Solstice, the Sun is in the constellation of the Tropic of Cancer, with a crab as its symbol. The constellation was named some 2000 years ago. So, keep in mind that, as everything in our dynamic universe is on the move, so too have changes occurred on the Earth itself; the actual point of magnetic N and S is shifting slightly all the time due to the properties of the molten metal outer core of our planet. As a result, our visual perspective of the heavenly bodies within our Milky Way Galaxy is ever-changing, however imperceptibly. Similarly, in the Winter Solstice, the Sun in its perihelion had been in Capricorn, but now it is approaching Sagittarius because of the change in the Earth's axis of rotation over 2000+ years.

By designating certain repasts to particular times of the year, we are creating meaningful traditions that reflect, through symbol, the focus of our celebration of the life-sustaining Sun and its relation to our shared home and haven: our Earth, from which we are all derived.

To prepare the soft-shell crab, generally they are alive when we get them, so first I kill them in a humane way so they don't feel any pain. [According to the Humane Society and the Royal Society for the Prevention of Cruelty to Animals, first chill them and then remove both the rear and front nerve centers]. Then, it's a matter of cleaning them, removing the lungs and innards. They are prepared for grilling by basting them in olive oil, onion powder and garlic. Then I grill them on a low heat outside.

Besides the crab, one of the other foods that has become part of the traditional foods we enjoy for Summer Solstice is scallop bruschetta. For the scallop bruschetta, I cut a large-sized scallop cross-wise into three or four coin-shaped discs (like the Sun) that are sautéed to a golden brown and placed atop a typical bruschetta (salsa on a toasted slice of baguette). Thus, a visual symbol of the Sun, alongside the crab, a symbol of the Tropic of Cancer.

At this point in the growing season, our garden just has peas, beans, and salad greens. So, we traditionally will make a salad for the meal with greens from the garden. Some of our guests have been creative and brought wines that have names that are associated with the Sun or the Earth. [There is one vintner that makes "Tuscan Sun Wines" and there are several Prosecco wines with "sole" in the name or with the Sun on the bottle]. We also have some special plates and dishes (with Sun and crab themes) that we use that have been given as gifts over the years.

Once we sit down to eat, we will share a poem to mark the occasion.

FOOD AND RELIGIOUS TRADITIONS

The connection between traditional foods and religious or spiritual celebrations can be found in virtually all cultures. Some examples:

- Lentils are eaten in Italy at New Year's as symbols of prosperity and wealth.

- Eastern European cultures have a pre-spring celebration (similar to the Catholic period of Lent) that involves eating pancakes to represent the Sun.

- The Passover Seder has the central "Seder plate" that includes matzah, the zeroa (shankbone), egg, bitter herbs, charoset paste and karpas vegetable, each possessing important symbolic value.

- The Mid-Autumn Festival, also known as the Mooncake Festival, is held on the 15th day of the eighth month in the Chinese calendar). Families gather to celebrate the year's harvest and make offerings to the Goddess of the Moon, Chang'e. Sweet mooncakes made from lotus paste with an egg yolk center are commonly eaten.

- Dwali, the Hindu celebration of the New Year, often includes sweet treats: Lapsi, and Puran Poli, breads that are cooked in butter (ghee) and sugar and enjoyed during the week-long celebration.

E.D.

Our special foods and special dishes

Scallop Bruschetta

Soft-shell Crab on the grill

Sun bowls

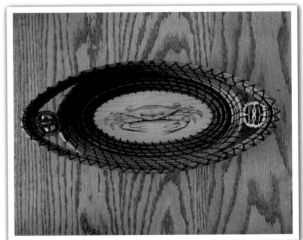

Crab basket
*(pine needle basket with black walnut decoration
made by Elaine Tanner with original wood-burn-
ing artwork by Ann F. Page--purchased in
South Carolina)*

45

"Summer in the South" by Paul Dunbar:

The Oriole sings in the greening grove
As if he were half-way waiting,
The rosebuds peep from their hoods of green,
Timid, and hesitating.
The rain comes down in a torrent sweep
And the nights smell warm and pinety,
The garden thrives, but the tender shoots
Are yellow-green and tiny.
Then a flash of sun on a waiting hill,
Streams laugh that erst were quiet,
The sky smiles down with a dazzling blue
And the woods run mad with riot.

The Summer Solstice Fire

Bonfires have long been part of communal cultural, historic, and religious celebrations around the world. There are several celebrations in England and Ireland that include bonfires, Guy Fawkes Night, St. John's Eve, and Halloween, for example. St. John's Eve, the celebration of the birth of the Christian St. John the Baptist and occurring at the time of Summer Solstice, has also been celebrated throughout history with outdoor fires in many other countries and cultures. The significance of the fires goes back to ancient times when they were lit to ward off evil spirits and bring good luck to the harvest.

E.D.

After the meal, as sunset approaches, we prepare for the Summer Solstice fire. A central part of both our Winter and Summer Solstice celebrations is the fire. The image of a fire, with its flickering light, can be mesmerizing and helps us to focus on our moments together during the gathering. We have both the Summer and Winter Solstice fires outside in a fire ring at the back of our yard. As you will read in the Winter Solstice chapter, during Winter Solstice, we consider the setbacks in our lives and the troublesome, burdensome, or self-defeating/self-sabotaging thoughts that we wish to be rid of. The symbolic act of writing these down and folding them into our Solstice wreath to be burned is a symbolic gesture of ridding these from our psyches. For the Summer Solstice fire, however, we contemplate our hopes for our lives during the continuing cycle and write these down, and throw them in the fire, in a symbolic gesture of having those hopes rise into the stratosphere. To distinctly distill the thought into words can be an inspiring personal act toward attaining a goal.

Right after dinner, we will listen to music and take time to reflect as we write down the hopes to be kindled. We gather by the fire, and we toss them in as we feel that we are connected to the idea of our hopes being fulfilled and trying our best to believe that this hope may arise, even in the knowledge that hopes often require planning and strategy and persistence to be achieved. The symbol of this is the rising smoke, the dissipating vapors rising like a prayer that asks for nothing, but rather reaches, like meditation, into our minds, and enables us to visualize a sought-after enriching condition for our lives, as well as for the lives of those that we love and care about. Generally, those moments of people connecting with their hopes and tossing them into the fire is a solemn time and may last five minutes or more. We sometimes will share these words after the hopes have all been placed into the fire:

We celebrate this, the longest day,
Grateful for the Sun's early light on the ocean,
Grateful for the fun of discovering wildflowers in fields and woods,
Grateful for the first summer and late spring foods,
Grateful to be all together once again to celebrate
  this still point in the turning year.

Even after, we may remain in silence and enjoy the fire. Inevitably, conversation ensues, there's laughter, and the exchange of ideas and stories. We will stay by the fire for a while, and then everyone eventually will disperse.

We hope to end the day with a new perspective, as we continue on our way in the cycles of our world, and we feel the strengthening bonds with those who share the orbits of support in our lives. We feel more connected than we were before.

Winter Solstice

Our Most Important Celebration of the Year

*Our Winter Solstice Wall-hanging
wood carving and painting by Jim T. Donovan*

Our Winter Solstice celebration begins at sunset and ends some time after sunrise the next day. Here lies a challenge: the wakeful witnessing of the entire longest night.

Our Winter Solstice Celebration Includes:

- Placing of the Solstice Wreath
- Lighting of the Solstice Candle at sunset.
- Winter Solstice Dinner
- Activities and music, and the making of the ornaments
- Preparing the luminaries
- Writing of the "burdens" and the Winter Solstice fire
- More activities
- Watching the sunrise
- Winter Solstice Breakfast
- Decorating of the holly tree.

Our Winter Solstice celebration begins with the wreath, taking it from where it has been decoratively displayed since the Summer Solstice and placing it in a prominent place for the celebration, which will revolve around sunset and sunrise and the burning of the wreath. Our wreath is weaved from grapevines in February or March, decorated with local wildflowers on the Summer Solstice, June 21st, and has been displayed in our sunporch ever since that time. What a colorful jubilee of arranged wildflowers intertwined within the grapevines it was! Now extremely dried and lacking its former vibrancy, it stands ready to serve as a testament to the ephemerality of the creations of Nature and the transformation of all things through time. It also serves as a reminder to strive for the ability to achieve a sense of non-attachment—to loosen any sense of grasping possessions, and to concentrate rather on experience and sharing. For, one can imagine, it required a lot of work to cut and intertwine these grapevines, and then for all of us to gather and arrange all these wildflowers. Even dried out, it is a thing of beauty. You'd pay a pretty penny for it in a novelty store or antique shop or on eBay. We as a group will remember our Summer Solstice time together this cold Winter Solstice as we convey it along a luminary-lighted path to the fire ring and sacrifice it as the symbolic vehicle which will convey our burdens up, up and away in its smoky transformation to smoldering ash.

The Solstice Candle

This time in the Northern Hemisphere is generally referred to as a "holiday of lights" and so it is that many cultures in the Northern Hemisphere have holidays and traditions at this time of year that feature candles and/or lights. Our Solstice candle turned out to be a rediscovery of a practice that apparently is inherent in nearly every culture. We simply wanted to mark the beginning of the longest night by lighting a candle. We have a specifically designated candle that is only lit on the longest night and we blow it out after returning from watching the sunrise the following morning. Then, we store it carefully until next year. Once we formally began to celebrate the Solstice, rather than just letting it come and go, we purchased this large, unique-looking candle, one we thought would safely and slowly burn through the long night. Our first candle was large (12"), green, and angular, tapering from bottom to top. The green, of course, symbolized the idea of "ever-green."

Over the years of using the same candle, it took on a sculpture-like appearance. Interestingly, that first candle, if you looked at it at its base, was in the design of the Star of David, hearkening to the Judaic tradition of the menorah, which is utilized in cultural tradition of

Festivals of Light from Around the World

Diwali in India: one of the most important celebrations in India, it celebrates the triumph of light over darkness, good over evil. People decorate their homes, light many lanterns and candles, and give out treats. It lasts for five days, and is in October or November.

St. Lucia's Day in Sweden: a wreath of candles is made as a gift to St. Lucia, on the longest night of the year

St. Martin's Day (Sint Maarten) in Holland: in November, children walk from house to house with lanterns singing songs and receive gifts and treats.

Loi Krathong (loy-kruh-thong) Festival in Thailand: in November people create sailing vessels out of banana leaves and fill them with candles, coins and joss-sticks and light the candles, setting the boats afloat in a river. The vessels supposedly carry away bad luck.

E.D.

Hanukah, celebrated at this same time of year, though for a professed different reason and purpose.

When we light the candle, we always have our first reading to set the tone, mood, and purpose for the all-night observance.

Reading for Lighting the Solstice Candle

Once again, the Winter Solstice is upon us. This is the time of year when we learn from the Earth how to face the darkness without losing hope, how to honor the fading light, and how to nurture the seeds of rebirth. We pause and reflect on the year now passed, with gratitude for all that has come into our lives. We think of those we have lost with love and respect.

We will face the longest night with the faith that, even in the darkest hour, there is a strength within us that we can draw upon until the light returns to us again.

Our Solstice Candle
Photograph by Becca Magrino

Winter Solstice Dinner

Just as many holidays and festivals involve, if not revolve around (no pun intended), food, the meals are an important facet of our celebration. However, particularly for the Winter Solstice, we strive to keep the meals simple. We hope to have the focus remain on the *event* rather than on the meal, as is the case in such traditional gatherings as Thanksgiving, 7 Fishes, and Passover, for example. One practical result of this practice is that, by restricting our caloric intake on the night, our bodies are not struggling to digest food, allowing for a more stable state of alertness, and this lends a more level perspective on our shared moments together and for the ideas, symbols, and phenomena we are exploring. Even so, even a simple meal requires some "prep," whether that be to previously purchase supplies, slice or mince vegetables, measure out spices, etc. Some foods can be totally pre-cooked, whereas others are best made fresh. The meals are always a group, or at least a shared, effort, but I really enjoy cooking (and experimenting while cooking), so a good portion of the menu is up to me. Primarily, I want to be a part of the gathered group and to be able to focus on reconnecting with or meeting new friends, so I'll do as much prep ahead of time without compromising on the quality of our fare.

There are a few menu items that have gained "tradition" status, even if they're not identical to past dishes. For example, we begin the meal with a simple consommé. Actually, two consommés, since one pot will be vegetarian broth and the other chicken—or bone-based.

Another traditional menu item is our rice/bean loaf. The purpose was to be able to serve a lot of people and to keep it simple. We want to use staples of many cultures, so we make it of beans and rice; combined, they create a "complete protein" in the meal. Note: In order to get the greatest nutrition out of beans and rice, cultures have come up with ways to prepare them so as to reduce any toxic elements.

So, we strive to adhere to best practices in cooking these ingredients together.

Though this is but one of our side dishes, it also serves as yet another opportunity to extend the symbolism of the celebration: we use a bundt cake mold that is hollow in the center so as to create a wreath-like ring. Though it's a simple food, it becomes a creative endeavor to have a finished product that contains so many symbolic elements, using the colors of red and green and using so many layers.

THE SIGNFICANCE OF RED AND GREEN

Modern humans have always associated the color green with growth and new life. The trees and plants that remain green year-round have served as symbols of the never-ending cycle of life on Earth. As for the importance of the combination of the two colors of red and green at winter time, there are many theories as to how that significance has evolved. Christian mythology holds that the color of red at Christmas represents the blood of Jesus. 20th century pop culture ascribes the prevalence of red at Christmas time to early Coca Cola ads that allegedly were the first portrayals of Santa Claus in a completely red suit. There are other theories more closely connected to celebrations of the Solstice. In ancient Celtic times, people would bring holly branches into their homes at the time of the Winter Solstice in order to remind them of the Earth's return to life in the spring. In late fall, holly trees are usually covered in red berries, so the holly branch offers the beautiful contrast of bright red with deep evergreen. Winter is also the time when male red-colored cardinals appear most striking against the evergreen tree branches. Red is the color associated with the element of fire, and green is associated with the element of earth, so their significance at Solstice can be seen to highlight the life-giving connection between the Sun and the Earth.

E.D.

So, to decoratively place red kidney beans, along with green peas also carefully placed, takes some doing, as does having "layers" or "orbits" of one layer of brown rice and some peas, another one having white rice and parsley, another of basmati rice and minced parmesan cheese with the kidney beans and peas appearing on top. What is going to be on top has to be placed in the mold first, of course. Everything then has to be very carefully, almost intricately, placed in the mold, red beans placed side by side in the ring, and then green peas being placed next to them. Then, the final layer of rice has to be placed so that it does not disturb that arrangement.

These are very simple foods, staples of so many societies and cultures. Here again, we have taken to making two versions, one with tiny squares of parmesan cheese interspersed and one without cheese at all so that those who are lactose-intolerant or vegan can enjoy this as well. One of the fun parts of making this dish happens at the moment of having it fall cleanly and fully intact from the mold—or not! Either way, there are always cheers, laughter, and/or feigned jeers.

Rice Loaf

Another tradition has been the main dish: baked sole. Ok, it's not spelled the same, but the name Sol is the Latin name of the Roman god of the Sun; its Greek counterpoint is Helios. So, really, we first chose sole fish for the fun of it, to lend a little bit more symbolism to all the other symbolic aspects of our celebrations. We usually bake the sole with a little butter or olive oil and lemon, some pepper and parsley and that's about it.

As with any fete, beverages will be a big factor for the enjoyment of your celebrations, and for our purposes, they lend yet another opportunity to have some fun with symbolism to focus on the point of the gathering. Frankly, the extent to which a person will be able to stay alert for the longest night of the year will be contingent on what he/she eats and drinks, so while I might choose to abstain from alcoholic or sweet drinks for the evening, no dictates are imposed upon anyone's preferences or desires, of course. To each his own, as it were. But heck, not everyone is able to stay for the entire night and some have designated drivers, so have some fun and try some theme drinks, alcoholic or virgin, to your liking.

Some suggestions to look up:

Alcoholic: Tequila Sunrise, Beach House Cosmos, The Sun Also Rises, Sun Beam, Sun Drop.
Non-alcoholic: Sunset, Arizona Sunset, Caribbean Sunset, Lime Sunset, Tropical Sunset

---

When we call everyone to the table, we sit and hold hands, and each will share a simple statement about the things for which he/she is grateful. [We actually do this at every nightly meal as a family. We started this when the children were little to help them be more conscious of "moments" and the idea of gratitude] Before serving, we have the opportunity for each guest to have a reckoning of the things in life we tend to take for granted: our health, our hands, our sound roof, being all together, even things as mundane as shoes; therefore it always lends itself to warmth, laughter, and sometimes a little "choking up." And, it's always fun to get the younger children involved, as they can sometimes be so silly when taking part in an activity that may be new to them. Sometimes they may even need a little coaching and guidance through questioning (e.g. do you have a favorite toy? A favorite book?) We also will ask everyone to focus on their five senses when exploring what they are most grateful for: the sights, the sounds, the smells, the tastes, the touches. After sharing our gratefulness, we may have another reading. And then dinner is served!

Activities After Dinner:

We live in the part of the country, central NJ coast, where the American holly tree is fairly common. We have several in our backyard. As this tree is "evergreen," it serves symbolically to represent the idea of continuing life in the starkest and darkest and coldest of times. After dinner, we begin the activity of making natural decorations for that tree. The idea is to connect with Nature. Our readings focused on symbolism, on our human sense of wonder and search for meaning, and on the science [astrophysical] of the Earth's relationship to the Sun. Now, this portion of the celebration is about having an awareness of our personal and communal relationship to Nature and the natural environment. And, we feel that by decorating our holly tree with decorations that are edible to animals, we are acknowledging our relationship to animals outside of our species. We are all creatures of this Earth and we all are dependent on biodiversity. So, this is just one symbolic act (decorating the tree) to help the animals through these long, cold winter days. Sitting in our living room by the fire, we will make: suet seed balls, popcorn strings, braided dried Siberian Iris reeds strung with cranberries, pretzels, or some type of oat cereal. Before or after making decorations we also engage in other activities.

Possible activities:

Acting out or pantomime a play about how animals in Nature will prepare for winter

Fun quizzes: ask people to answer a series of questions about their experience of the year gone by, leaving off their names (What was the best thing that happened to you this year? What are you most proud of? What was the biggest challenge you overcame this year? If you could name a Person of the Year, who would that be? What is your dream for the next year?); shuffle and pass the answer sheets around to be read aloud as everyone tries to guess who wrote those answers

Have a sing-along: simple drumming, maybe a guitar playing a simple blues riff, as the group chants "Let it Go". People take turns improvising a verse in which they share a troubling/frustrating experience they had recently, and after each verse, the group goes back to the refrain of "let it go."

For more activity ideas, visit seasonsinmind.com

E.D.

Preparing the Luminaries

We have adopted a tradition of creating a luminary-lighted path from the house to the backyard holly tree and campfire ring. Making the luminaries is a fun activity for the older kids or teenagers to engage in, usually right before our dinner, although sometimes, they do it right afterward, or both. The luminaries are simple brown paper lunch bags, their tops folded over to keep the bag open, secured by the gravity of a cup or so of fresh dry cat litter placed inside and a tea candle laid on top.

We make as many as 50 or so of these luminaries. Then, we create a meandering, serpentine path of them, spaced 10-12 feet/3-4 meters apart to lead us to the holly tree and campfire ring.

A Luminary

The Walk

For many, the experience of the serene nighttime walk along the candlelit path is the most moving, and some have said "spiritual," part of our event, perhaps second only to the "burning of the burdens," to be described later on. Ideally, you will have a long-armed butane lighter or two to light each candle at the prescribed time. Best-case scenario is for there to be no artificial electrical lighting in the area, thus lending a greater opportunity to experience the celestial atmosphere above, along with the swirling river of candlelight that seems to reflect the distant night sky. Your eyes adjust quickly to the dim and distant flickering rays, and you can almost feel your heart quicken, your pupils broaden, as when one comes into the presence of one adored. A peaceful feeling sets in. With each step, there's a sudden sense of being a part of something huge, vast and open. The silence and the chilly breezes seem to hold a message, a calling, an invitation. Walking with scribbled burdens on little folded pieces of paper, we prepare to make a new commitment to ourselves, to bring change into our lives, to create a clean slate and a sense of purity.

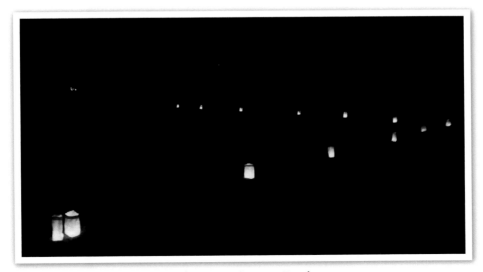

The Luminary Path

Writing of the "Burdens" and the Winter Solstice Fire

It is the longest night of the year; almost precisely sixteen hours, so at the mid-point of the longest night we enter into the most solemn and introspective portion of the celebration. We call it the "burning of the burdens," a symbolic act of writing on individual little pieces of paper these personal burdens that hold us back.

This night holds so much gravity for us that we treat it as others might a major holiday—we inform the schools that our children will not be attending the next day and make plans for them to make up any missed work.

E.D.

We each identify particular things prohibiting us from being completely in the moment, from being happy, and from having an abiding sense of fulfillment in our one-and-only life. Sometimes these are particular concerns or worries. Sometimes they are reactions to the increasingly frantic pace of life, or behaviors we feel have become negative habits. Essentially, it comes down to burdens that are limiting or prohibiting our ability to find greater personal fulfillment, greater awareness, so as to become more attuned in our personal relationships, bringing perspective to life's obligations and achieving an orderliness to proceed ahead. We have created an activity that, here again, reflects many social and religious practices that have come to be in many cultures and organized religions. We take this opportunity to identify those elements in our life that are inhibiting our betterment, our happiness, our feelings of satisfaction in many facets of our lives. These are very personal ideas and are shared with no one. Burdens are written individually on small pieces of paper, folded up and pocketed until the time we bring the wreath to the backyard fire ring (some of us fold the papers and insert them deep into the weaves of the wreath ahead of time), where we will engage in yet another symbolic act of sacrifice and renewal. The sacrifice is symbolized by the burning of the wreath itself. All of our efforts to make it a beautiful artistic creation will now go up in smoke, symbolizing our willingness toward detachment and the acceptance of ephemeral Nature. The renewal comes in the belief that we each will start afresh.

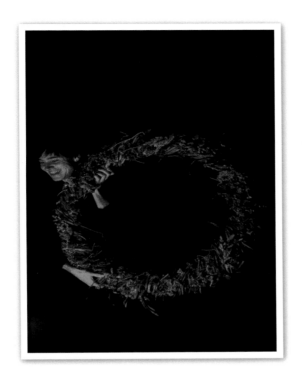

Placing the Wreath on the Solstice Fire
Photographs by Becca Magrino

It's a solemn, quiet time, each of us standing side by side, lit only by the flickering flames of this healing fire. Setting the wreath alight, the conflagration rising, we consider again the words on each scrap of paper and endeavor to believe that this burden may be symbolically lifted from our being, rising in the smoke, up and away from us into the glowing cinders rising into the starry night. For some, this is the culmination of the evening, and so some will shortly thereafter go home: some people have to go to work the next morning, after all. Many of us will continue to witness the longest night, lingering by the fire, engaging in extemporaneous conversation, and then will return to the house in dribs and drabs, singularly, in couples or in groups, walking again along the lighted path. Back at the house, dishes will be cleaned, and the kitchen straightened, the making of the edible ornaments will re-commence, and some will sit quietly and read. The teenagers love to read aloud from the *Weird NJ* books on Solstice night—these stories are just creepy and entertaining enough to keep them awake and alert. The kids also sometimes go back outside into the cold and sometimes snowy darkness. Others will take an opportunity to find a place in the house to do a focused meditation. Some may opt to forego the all-night vigil and choose to take a nap in a guest room, with a request for a wake-up in time for sunrise. Particularly in a place where one feels a sense of belonging and freedom from judgement, there's a phenomenon when fatigue and sleeplessness, hand-in-hand with a sense of calm and contentment, can lend itself to a psychic state whereupon deep-seated tensions are allowed to breach the surface of our inhibited self and can find expression in varying ways, whether it be in uncontrolled giddiness or laughter, quiet and sometimes emotional sharing, or even a sense of euphoria and bliss. It's not unusual for some to feel inspired and will go sit alone and start writing, whether it be poetry, a letter, or lyrics, or the like.

Watching the Sunrise

At the first hints of dawn, as the stars begin to fade and the eastern horizon begins to glow, excitement swells for those who stayed awake the whole night. One of our traditions has been to enliven the house with strains of Neil Diamond's "Holly Holy" which begins with a sleepy, tinny guitar strum above what sounds like a throbbing washtub base rhythm, his sultry vocal entrance, supported by a muscular piano, joined by a tambourine and a choir, building inexorably, soaring with the sounds of strings, and eliciting images of a "coming" and of running and of flying and of the elation of a gospel chorus. It exudes the power of a man struggling to walk against ocean waves. It's a great "wake-up song." It's an effective motivator because it begins with a pleasant beckoning and soon gets you on your feet. We feel that this song is about Solstice: holly is the evergreen plant and the tree we decorate; holly is the symbol of everlasting life. His description of the "seed full with tomorrow" embodies the promise and newness that we hope to achieve having symbolically jettisoned our burdens during the longest night.

We live in a place where the most advantageous viewing spot is not within walking distance, so we have to drive about eight minutes. We need to figure how many vehicles we'll need to take and how many people we can fit into each car. The coffee is perking, and people need time to have a cup. These moments

> Other songs to get into the spirit of the morning are "Circle of Life" "Oh Joyful Children" "Walk Right Up to the Sun" and Emilia Donovan's "I Believe in the Rising Sun."

allow us to become motivated and psyched for the sunrise. This is the long-awaited culmination of the longest night.

The quality of the sunrise is always a variable, and frankly, quite a crap-shoot. If we're lucky, it's not overcast. If it's snowing or raining, we'll just "observe" at home. Sometimes, the Sun will be visible coming over the horizon just before it disappears into the low-hanging clouds. As the sailors' saying goes: "red in the morning, sailors warning; red at night, sailors delight." While red in the morning may be harbinger of bad weather ahead, we are grateful to be able to experience at least some degree of the sunrise. Over the past twenty-five years of celebrating the Solstice, we have been able to see a sunrise more often than not. And so, it has been worth bundling up and loading into the car, some groggily, driving over hill and dale to reach the destination from which we will walk uphill to a clearing that gives us the perfect vantage point to the southeast.

On *this* day, what we're calling **Winter Solstice**, the North Pole is pointing in its most opposite direction away from the Sun. However, the Sun will rise just a little more south for a couple more weeks until *perihelion* when the Earth is actually at the end of its elliptical path around the Sun, the true "Sun stop" and the Earth's closest annual proximity to the Sun (*aphelion* is when Earth is at the other end of its path but farthest from the Sun, in June/July). So, to be clear, the **first day of Winter** is when the Earth's *axis* is *point*ing farthest from the Sun, and *perihelion* is when the Earth is in its closest position to the Sun on its elliptical path. This relationship changes over the eons, so we're grateful in the knowledge that these points are presently so close in time.

So, why is this relationship changing over the eons? It is fascinating to think about how the Earth's axis is "wobbling" (gradually circling like a slowing spinning top) and will eventually change the relationship between the moment of the beginning of the winter season (what is called "Solstice" which means "Sun stop") and the moment of perihelion (which is actually when the Sun seems to "stop" as the Earth begins its return voyage on its elliptical path). As a result, in about 7000 years, what humanity has been calling "Winter Solstice," correlating to when the Earth's axis is pointing away from the Sun, will occur when Earth is in a different place on its elliptical path, where it is now in the month of March, presently our Equinox. It's really just coincidence that as human civilization was forming, the seasons aligned with the perihelion and aphelion.

Additionally, the full cycle of axial "wobble" (*precession*) takes almost 26,000 years and affects Earthlings in their perspective of the "North Star." Right now, the North Star is Polaris, in the constellation Ursa Minor, but in 13,000 years, it will be Vega, the brightest star in the constellation Lyra. This knowledge lends itself as fodder for our sense of wonder (if not your sense of confusion, lol)!

Winter Solstice Sunrise

As locations go regarding witnessing a sunrise, you may be more fortunate than we. The Sun is rising at its most southerly-eastward point, and from perihelion on, it will rise a little more northward in the eastern sky. So, while this might be a good spot for the Winter Solstice, it may be a terrible spot to watch the Summer Solstice sunrise. If we want to watch the Sun rise over the ocean, we would have to drive twenty minutes to Sandy Hook, NJ, which is not feasible for a large group so early in the morning having stayed up all night. Our most advantageous location situates us on a hill looking across to yet another hill. So, while the actual sunrise in our area may be 7:20, we won't actually see it until 7:45. Our spot is convenient, though not the most aesthetic. We're in a high clearing just below the Horn Antenna and looking beyond the distant giant transistor-shaped water tower at the former Bell Labs and at a point where the Garden State Parkway disappears over the horizon about three miles away.

Climbing the hill, with the brightening sky, we quicken our pace so as to not miss the moment of sunrise, but we invariably have quite a few minutes of waiting before the moment occurs. It's important to remember to bring your sunglasses. While the thickness of the atmosphere may color the sunrise in a spectacular way, the lensing effect can surely damage your eyes. There is always a sense of accomplishment

The **Holmdel Horn Antenna**, designated a national historic landmark in 1988, was the location where Nobel Prize -winning scientists Arno Penzias and Robert Wilson detected the cosmic microwave background radiation that confirmed the big bang theory of the origin of our universe.

and privilege in witnessing the sunrise because not everyone is in a place to be cognizant of the moment or to have a clear view of it. It's also our reward for having stayed up all night, a reward with lasting effects, as the company of people coming together is always a variable, so there is a sense of gratitude for being able to share these moments together, some of them for the first time. So, we take an opportunity for some photography and we make our way back to the cars and to our house.

Watching the Sunrise

At the Horn Antenna
(presently facing downward)

Winter Solstice Breakfast

Once back at the house, we will gather at the Solstice candle. Sometimes we will have a reading or sing yet another song before having one of the children then extinguish the flame that has been burning all night. It's fun to think about how perhaps at the dawn of language, the earliest modern humans would tell children cautionary stories about the possibility of the nights getting longer and longer, as though the Sun were escaping the sky, only to let them discover for themselves that the Sun had stopped moving southward and had begun its trek northward in the eastern sky, thus bringing back the longer days and presaging the time to sow seeds. It's an interesting contrast between what a child knows about today in this technological age compared to the knowledge generally acquired by children in that most natural setting of ancient times. This is why it's fun to be around children experiencing the sunrise on Winter Solstice—the witnessing of the birth of a new day is a memorable delight.

After extinguishing the candle, we pause for one more song "Cycles" by Frank Sinatra. The title lends itself to the idea of the cycles of the season, but in the song it's a manifestation of our having to deal with the lows as well as enjoying the highs inherent in a lifetime. It's quite a touching song, though in some regards, "kind of funny."

Now, we make breakfast. To remind us of the coming Summer Solstice, I make crabmeat omelets, the crab symbolizing that at Summer Solstice, the Sun will be in the Tropic of Cancer, or we continue the Sun theme with sunny-side up eggs or garnishes that elicit the Sun. At breakfast we have a reading.

Reading for Solstice Breakfast

Let's pause and think about how we feel on this new morning.

When we reflect back on the many emotions we might have felt over the longest night: joy, gratitude, love, hospitality, and maybe loneliness, loss, or even despair, and we think about the burdens we hope we have now shed, our hearts and minds are full. We may feel the season's promise of hope and redemption, yet we know that redemption does not come to us according to any schedule or calendar. It is up to us to make our meaning out of Solstice, and each year, we may surprise ourselves with how Solstice has changed us, although we may not see that change until far into this new year.

We savored the long night, the moments of festivity and the moments of calm. But this longest night is now over and our breakfast feast has begun. After we rest, and then decorate the holly tree, night will fall again. We will take comfort in this season's gifts and the gifts of each other, having embraced the darkness together and having risen to celebrate the new day.

E.D.

Decorating the Tree

After breakfast, we are all generally in a state of almost a psychological lull, a sense of satiety and relaxation. We have one last task: to decorate the tree with the edible ornaments. We gather them up and get to work. The American Holly tree in our yard has grown quite large in the past several years, and we decorate the tree. It's a fun group activity because we have a lot of laughs about how some of these ornaments have turned out—some of them are pretty funny-looking: popcorn strings with only a cranberry or two; braided iris strands that hold just fragments of pretzel that broke in the process; while others are quite creative or artistic feats, a clear testament to one's ability to focus their creativity on the task of making the ornaments. Most are quite simple: strings of popcorn or strings of o-shaped oat cereal with dried cranberries or braided iris strands holding pretzels.

Decorating the Tree

For more pictures of decorations visit seasonsinmind.com

Once we're done decorating, I share a final reading that has been one of the most traditional of all of our readings, having read it at our very first celebration and every one thereafter. It includes an excerpt from William Wordsworth's "Ode: Intimations of Immortality" and some final words of my own:

"Though nothing can bring back the hour
Of splendour in the grass, of glory in the flower;
We will grieve not, rather find
Strength in what remains behind;
In the primal sympathy
Which having been must ever be;
In the soothing thoughts that spring
Out of human suffering;
In the faith that looks through death,
In years that bring the philosophic mind."

And so we begin again on a journey that the ancients knew
But which was lost
And which we discover again
That we are creatures of the Earth
And that we can be grateful for the Sun
        which gives us life.
And with the ability of our minds, evolved,
We <u>know</u> that we love
We live
We think
We know
We love.

With this, we have earned a sense of peace and tranquility as we move forward into the new calendar year. Having become conscious of our relationship to the Earth and beyond, we live with a year-round relationship to the seasons and are in a continual state of looking forward to the next phase of our understanding.

Acknowledgements

We want to thank the following people who have contributed to and invested so much thought and enthusiasm in the development of this project:

Emilia Donovan for being a central part of our celebrations since her birth and for sharing her songs at Winter Solstice each year.

Harriman Donovan for being a central part of these celebrations since his birth and for his design of the book's cover and for his illustration of the Earth's elliptical path.

Becca Magrino for joining us in many of the celebrations and for her beautiful photographs of Winter Solstice.

We want to thank those who have shared in our celebrations from the earliest days: John Cozza, James Dievler, Joe Duncan, Larry and Anne Fink, Carl Mastropaolo, and Rachel Scher.

Thank you to Katy Cedano for reading a draft of the manuscript and offering her helpful feedback.

References

These are resources we have found that might be helpful in pursuing further information and ideas on the Solstices. Other resources are cited in the individual sidebars within the text.

Book resources:

Heinberg, Richard. *Celebrate the Solstice: Honoring the Earth's Seasonal Rhythms through Festival and Ceremony.* Wheaton, IL: Quest Books/The Theosophical Publishing House, 1993. This book provides a history of seasonal celebrations from ancient times and offers a guide to present day festivals

Kingsolver, Barbara. *Animal, Vegetable, Miracle: A Year of Food Life*. NY: Harper Collins Publishers, 2007. This book describes a year in Kingsolver's family's life when they chose to eat only foods available locally and seasonally. Offers ideas on how to incorporate this practice into your life and provides abundant research to support the value of this practice.

Leslie, Clare Walker and Frank E. Gerace. *The Ancient Celtic Festivals*. Rochester, VT: Inner Traditions International, 2000. This children's book describes the ancient Celtic culture and its festivals and offers modern ways to recreate those celebrations.

Matthews, John. *The Winter Solstice: The Sacred Traditions of Christmas*. Wheaton, IL: Quest Books/The Theosophical Publishing House, 1998. This book provides lots of information on the origins of winter holiday celebrations and contains ideas for creating your own celebrations.

National Audubon Society Field Guide to the Night Sky

Villegas, Teresa. *How to Celebrate the Winter Solstice*. Heart and Mind Press, 2014. This book provides a brief explanation of the solstices and describes some ways to celebrate the occasion.

Ellen Jackson has a series of children's books on seasonal celebrations that include information and stories that can be used as part of your own celebrations.

Web Resources:

Gardenguides.com

Old Farmer's Almanac: almanac.com

Pennsylvania State University Extension: https://extension.psu.edu   Great source of information on trees and plants

Washington State University Extensions: https://extension.wsu.edu   Great searchable database of horticultural articles